KU-015-350

CONTENTS

THE AI-DRIVEN LIFE

At exactly 7.00 a.m., your eyes flutter open. The sound of your favourite song fills your ears. Your bedroom blinds slide open. The music slowly grows louder until you are wide awake.

You dress and brush your teeth. After rushing downstairs, you grab a glass of orange juice. You put the empty container on the worktop and rush out of the door. While you're gone your house-bot will clean the worktops and floors. And your fridge will place an order for more juice for the next morning.

Your mum has already gone to work. A driverless car is waiting for you outside the front door. You slip into the backseat, and the car heads to school. It chooses a route that avoids traffic jams and roadworks. After it drops you off, the car texts your mum to let her know that you have arrived safely.

Does all of this sound too good to be true? It isn't. Thanks to artificial intelligence (AI), people may see all of these things and more in the very near future.

THE WORLD OF ARTIFICIAL INTELLIGENCE

ARTIFICIAL INTELLIGENCE
AT HOME AND ON THE GO

BY TAMMY ENZ

raintree

a Capstone company — publishers for children

Raintree is an imprint of Capstone Global Library Limited, a company incorporated in England and Wales having its registered office at 264 Banbury Road, Oxford, OX2 7DY – Registered company number: 6695582

www.raintree.co.uk
myorders@raintree.co.uk

Edited by Karen Aleo and Christopher Harbo
Designed by Brann Garvey
Original illustrations © Capstone Global Library Limited 2020
Picture research by Pam Mitsakos and Tracy Cummins
Production by Kathy McColley
Originated by Capstone Global Library Ltd
Printed and bound in India

ISBN 978 1 4747 8179 4 (paperback)   ISBN 978 1 4747 7105 4 (paperback)
23 22 21 20 19   23 22 21 20 19
10 9 8 7 6 5 4 3 2 1   10 9 8 7 6 5 4 3 2 1

British Library Cataloguing in Publication Data
A full catalogue record for this book is available from the British Library.

Acknowledgements
We would like to thank the following for permission to reproduce photographs: Alamy: picturelibrary, 21; Getty Images: Kyodo News, 12, Westend61, 18; Shutterstock: BlueSkyImage, 14, Casimiro PT, 9, ID1974, 26-27, Mangostar, 8, metamorworks, 13, 20, 22, Miriam Doerr Martin Frommherz , 4-5, Montri Nipitvittaya, 16, nd3000, 6-7, Nopparat Angchakan, 15, panuwat phimpha, 17, PaO_STUDIO, Cover, pathdoc, 28-29, Peshkova, 19, Ralf Gosch, 24, Supphachai Salaeman, Design Element, Zapp2Photo, 10-11, 23. The publisher does not endorse products whose logos may appear on objects in images in this book.

Every effort has been made to contact copyright holders of material reproduced in this book. Any omissions will be rectified in subsequent printings if notice is given to the publisher.

CHAPTER 1

HOW AI WORKS

People have programmed computers to perform tasks for years. But artificial intelligence moves beyond that. AI allows machines to solve problems and perform tasks that would normally require human intelligence.

But machines don't develop AI by themselves. People create software that helps AI systems learn. This software can **analyse** large amounts of data. Then it **predicts** what will happen based on the information it has received. The more information AI analyses, the better its predictions become.

analyse examine something carefully in order to understand it

predict say what you think will happen in the future

Computer and robotics engineers create artificial intelligence software that allows robots to think for themselves.

Smartphones use AI to understand spoken words and turn them into text.

AI ON THE RISE

The idea that machines could learn to think for themselves has been around for decades. But the computing power needed for AI has only been developed recently. For instance, think about the voice-to-text feature on a smartphone. It's easy for your brain to understand spoken words and for you to write them down. But it takes a lot of processing power for a computer to understand spoken words and turn them into text.

FACT

Have you ever used Google Photos? It uses AI to recognize different images, tag people and store pictures by type.

AI is on the rise in other ways as well. Websites and credit card companies use AI to predict your spending habits. Amazon uses AI to learn what you like to buy and to recommend other products you might enjoy. Credit card companies use AI to prevent **fraud**. The software learns your shopping habits and sends you a message if it thinks someone else is using your credit card.

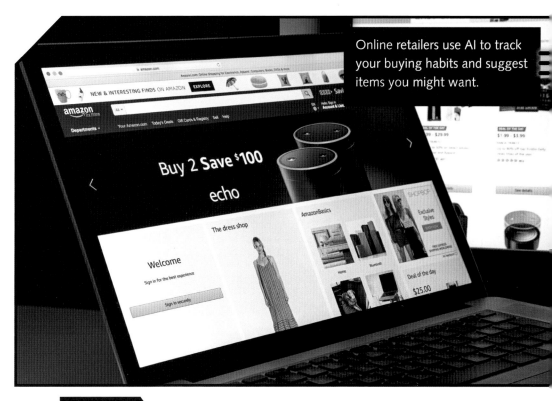

Online retailers use AI to track your buying habits and suggest items you might want.

FACT

The scientific study of artificial intelligence dates back more than 60 years. The Dartmouth Summer Research Project on Artificial Intelligence took place in 1956.

fraud cheating or tricking people

CHAPTER 2

AI AT HOME

When AI is connected to machines in your home, they gather information about you. As they learn what you like, they make your life easier. Here are a few of the common ways AI is changing how we live...

DIGITAL ASSISTANTS

What's the weather forecast for tomorrow? Is it going to rain? Should I take an umbrella? Imagine all the ways you can ask a question about the weather. Until recently, only humans could understand and answer these types of questions. But AI has changed that.

Siri, Alexa, Cortana and Google Assistant are popular digital assistants that use AI. These assistants understand your voice and use the internet to correctly answer thousands of questions. Are you trying to remember the title of a song? Just say a few lines. Then these assistants will name it and play it for you.

FACT

Some wireless earbuds now link to digital assistants such as Siri and Alexa.

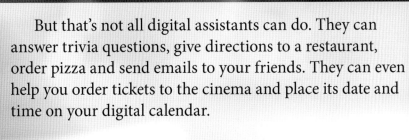

But that's not all digital assistants can do. They can answer trivia questions, give directions to a restaurant, order pizza and send emails to your friends. They can even help you order tickets to the cinema and place its date and time on your digital calendar.

Digital assistants also use AI to learn your likes and dislikes. Over time, they become better and better at suggesting music, films and restaurants you might like.

The Echo Dot allows users to ask Amazon's Alexa digital assistant to play music, read audio books and play trivia games.

SMART GADGETS

Digital assistants can do more than answer questions and keep your calendar up-to-date. They can help around the house by connecting to a variety of gadgets. For example, digital assistants can predict when you'll get home from school. Then they can adjust the heat and turn on the lights for you.

Home appliances are using artificial intelligence technology as well. LG's smart fridge has digital assistant capabilities. It can understand voice commands to create to-do lists and order food from the supermarket. It can also communicate with your smartphone.

LG's Smart InstaView fridge understands voice commands with the help of Amazon's Alexa.

FACT

The Google Clips camera uses AI. You can set it aside while you enjoy an activity. Then it decides when to take a photo.

Health Check

72 %

Weather
22°F 40%

SUN MON TUE WED THU FRI SAT

News

Smart mirrors may one day allow users to check their health, the weather and the news while getting ready for the day.

In the near future, your bathroom may even have AI. Kohler's smart mirror may one day include the digital assistant Alexa. With it you could watch the news as you get ready or give it voice commands to turn on the taps. Kohler has a toilet that responds to your voice too. It can follow commands to play music or even warm the seat!

AI CLEANS UP

AI is hard at work in many people's homes. Created in 2002, Roomba is an **autonomous** vacuum cleaner that travels around a house. It cleans carpets and floors. Roomba has simple **sensors** that find dirty areas. They also help the small robot move around furniture. No one has to be at home for Roomba to work.

autonomous able to carry out a job on one's own

sensor device that measures a physical property such as temperature or brightness

HOME SECURITY

Artificial intelligence can also make your home safer. Many home security systems use sensors to alert the police of a break-in. But AI uses **facial recognition** to identify family members. It even recognizes your dog. Smart security systems also let you know whenever a door or window is opened. The systems can call for help when they think a thief has broken in.

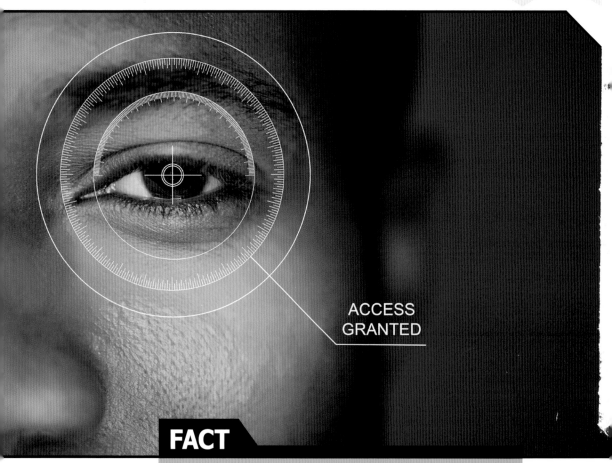

ACCESS
GRANTED

FACT

Iris scanners use AI to let you in and keep criminals out. If the scanner recognizes the unique pattern of your eye's iris, it will unlock the door.

AI-enhanced drones may one day keep an eye on our homes.

How might AI keep your home safe in the future? One way might be with AI drones equipped with cameras that hover over and watch your home. Another might be to scan security footage for suspicious activity. AI can do this task faster than humans. In this way, AI may be able to predict a crime and stop a break-in before it even happens.

facial recognition computer program that identifies people by the features of their faces

iris round, coloured part of your eye

Are you looking for Special Discount?

Some shops are developing smartphone apps that talk directly to customers and help them shop.

PERSONAL SHOPPERS

If AI can recognize you in your home, it may well be that department stores and other **retailers** will want to know who you are too. Some shops may one day use AI for facial recognition. By recognizing people as they enter a shop, the retailer can send messages directly to their smartphones. These messages will tell customers about products or sales that they might be interested in.

Other retailers are developing computer apps that talk directly to customers. These chatbots help people find clothing that fits their style or plan meals for the week.

AI could also help you find something when you don't know where to start looking. Imagine seeing someone on the street with a great pair of shoes or a cool T-shirt. Just snap a photo with a smartphone. An app like CamFind will tell you where to buy them.

FACT

The term "chatbot" is a combination of the words "chatter" and "robot".

retailer business that sells products to people for their own use

AI AND ONLINE SHOPPING

AI is already at work for online retailers. As you search for items, AI learns what you like and suggests other products you might want. But it won't stop there. Soon shopping sites may use technology that can tell how long you look at an image on a screen. They will then suggest products based on which items you looked at the longest.

AI may also make it possible to test products before buying them online. Using AI with **virtual reality** (VR) will allow shoppers to interact with objects by putting on VR goggles. Imagine seeing a toy or a jacket on a computer screen. VR might allow you to see how big the toy is in real life or what you look like wearing the jacket. AI will use everything it has learned about you to make your VR experience feel as real as possible.

A couple uses virtual reality goggles to experience the features of a new car.

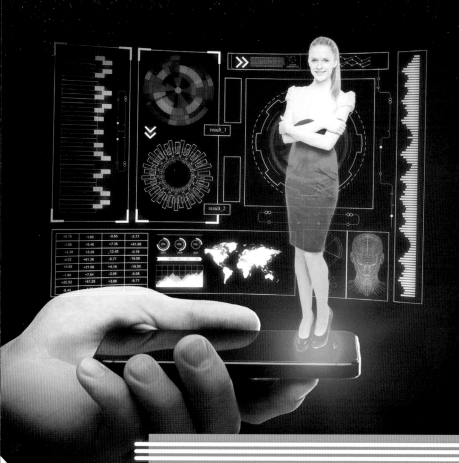

VIRTUAL
SALESPEOPLE

Imagine shopping with the help of a 3D image! In the future you may meet virtual salespeople. AI will use the information it has about you to make a **hologram** of a salesperson that you may enjoy interacting with to help you shop.

virtual reality computer-generated 3D world with which humans can interact

hologram image made by laser beams that looks three-dimensional

CHAPTER 3

AI ON THE GO

Imagine if you could get in a car and just tell it where you want to go. Then it studies traffic conditions to find the fastest route. It pulls on and off motorways and changes lanes. It even parks by itself. Do these abilities sound far-fetched? Companies such as Tesla, Google and Ford don't think so. They're already test-driving cars that can do all of these things and more.

In the future self-driving cars will navigate busy roads and motorways while their human passengers sit back and relax.

FACT

Car makers have high hopes for self-driving cars. Nearly every major car maker is developing one.

Self-driving cars need a lot of technology to drive safely. They use cameras and **radar** to see in 2D. **Lidar**, a laser sensor technology, allows the car to see even better in 3D.

But self-driving cars also need experience to predict what might happen on the road and drive safely. AI helps the cars learn how other cars move, how to stop quickly to avoid accidents and how to adjust their speed for the road conditions. The computer systems then use the collected data to make safe driving decisions on the road. And to gain all that experience, car makers test their self-driving cars on the road for hundreds of thousands of kilometres.

radar device that uses radio waves to track the location of objects

lidar device that measures the distance to an object by bouncing light off the object and timing how long it takes the light to return

SMART FEATURES

Actually owning a self-driving car may be several years away. However, many cars already have AI smart features in them. Parking assist can steer a car into or out of tight parking spaces. Some cars come with pre-crash warning systems that use cameras and sensors. If the driver fails to brake in time, the car will brake instead. Other systems spot objects the driver may not be able to see while reversing, such as children or cyclists.

AI systems are also making driving easier with internet-connected cars. Connected cars help drivers map their destinations, find restaurants or pay for fuel without leaving the car. AI can even alert garages when a car needs repairs and make an appointment.

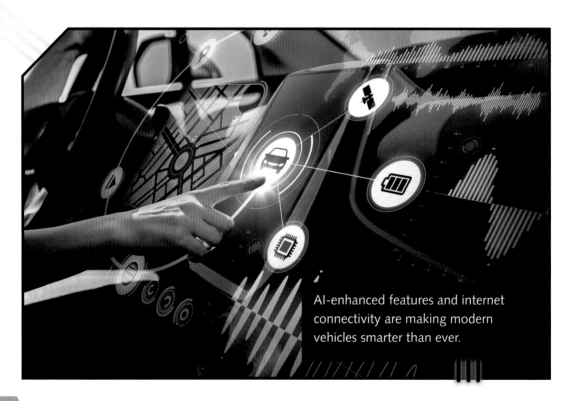

AI-enhanced features and internet connectivity are making modern vehicles smarter than ever.

CONNECTED CARS

Expect cars of the future to be fully connected to the internet. People will be able to interact with their cars the way they do their smartphones. They will be able to send messages and perform searches using their voices.

Artificial intelligence helps rush hour traffic flow more smoothly at some junctions.

AI AND TRAFFIC SAFETY

Artificial intelligence doesn't just make travel safer and easier in high-tech vehicles. It helps ordinary cars get around too. For instance, some traffic signals in Pittsburgh, Pennsylvania, USA, use an AI system to analyse traffic patterns.

The system, called Surtrac, uses a computer and a camera to watch cars approach a junction from all directions. The system then adjusts the timing of the traffic lights. By doing so, it helps vehicles flow as quickly as possible during the busiest times.

Surtrac helps traffic at more than just one place at a time. It also sends data to other connected junctions down the road. This data allows those junctions to plan for traffic heading their way. With the power of AI, Surtrac has reduced travel times by as much as 25 per cent along the routes on which it is used.

Pittsburgh has about 50 junctions equipped with Surtrac, with plans to expand to 200 in the coming years. Other cities in the United States also plan to add Surtrac to some of their road networks.

FACT

Ford has applied for a **patent** for a self-driving police car. The company believes the car may one day watch for speeders on its own. Then it will issue speeding tickets electronically.

patent legal document giving someone sole rights to make or sell a product

PLANES AND TRAINS

In the future, artificial intelligence won't be limited to road vehicles. AI may one day fly aeroplanes and operate trains too.

Autopilot has been used for decades, but human pilots are still needed to help fly planes. Even in the middle of a flight, pilots must keep an eye on wind speeds and take over during bad weather. But companies such as Airbus and Boeing have plans for planes that fly without human pilots. Airbus has designs for a self-flying air taxi called Vahana. The aircraft will fly up to 80 kilometres (50 miles) on its own. Boeing plans to build a fleet of commercial jetliners that use AI to fly themselves.

Artificial intelligence is also being developed to make train travel safer. In the future, trains with radar and lidar will look for objects on the track and decide how to handle the situation. These trains will also check weather conditions and adjust speeds to prevent accidents and reduce delays.

FACT

The company Kitty Hawk is working to get its self-flying air taxi approved for use in New Zealand. The aircraft, called Cora, is designed to take off and land in busy cities without a runway.

autopilot computer system that flies
a plane without human help

CHAPTER 4

WHAT COULD GO WRONG?

Artificial intelligence is enriching nearly every aspect of our lives. With so many uses, are there any downsides to this technology?

As with all new technologies, there are some issues. For instance, although digital assistants may use AI, they're not perfect. Sometimes they don't understand our requests, and they could hinder us more than they help. And what about the organizations that develop AI systems? Can we trust search engine companies not to use AI to influence voters by biasing the information they receive? Should we be concerned about countries wanting to use AI to more effectively control or attack other countries?

When it comes to travel, some people are unsure if we can trust computers to drive or fly better than humans. For instance, in March 2018 an experimental, self-driving car struck and killed a woman who was crossing the street. Both the car's self-driving system and the back-up human driver were found to be at fault for the crash. However, this type of accident makes people wonder if AI is worth the risks.

Many people rightly have concerns about AI and transport. But the future looks bright for AI. It already has the power to help us plan our days, make our homes safer and help us shop. One day it may even get us to a destination across the country without anyone controlling the vehicle. When it comes to artificial intelligence, there may be no limit to how smart our technology can become.

Our devices are getting smarter with artificial intelligence, but they don't always understand what we want them to do.

GLOSSARY

analyse examine something carefully in order to understand it

autonomous able to carry out a job on one's own

autopilot computer system that flies a plane without human help

facial recognition computer program that identifies people by the features of their faces

fraud cheating or tricking people

hologram image made by laser beams that looks three-dimensional

iris round, coloured part of your eye

lidar device that measures the distance to an object by bouncing light off the object and timing how long it takes the light to return

patent legal document giving someone sole rights to make or sell a product

predict say what you think will happen in the future

radar device that uses radio waves to track the location of objects

retailer business that sells products to people for their own use

sensor device that measures a physical property such as temperature or brightness

virtual reality computer-generated 3D world with which humans can interact

FIND OUT MORE

BOOKS

All About Virtual Reality, Jack Challoner (DK Children, 2017)

The Impact of Technology in Music (The Impact of Technology), Matthew Anniss (Raintree, 2016)

Robot: Meet the Machines of the Future, Laura Buller, Clive Gifford and Andrea Mills (DK Children, 2018)

WEBSITE

www.bbc.co.uk/newsround/27599859
Learn more about self-driving cars.

INDEX